20 Years of Broadside Copyright © 2006 by Jeffrey L. Bacon. All rights reserved. Printed in the United States of America. No part of this book may be reproduced or transmitted in any form or by any means, electronic or mechanical including photocopying, recording, or by any information storage and retrieval system without permission in writing from the Publisher, except in the case of reprints in the context of reviews. Contact Deep Water Publishing or admin@navybroadside.com for more information.

All situations depicted in this book are fictional. Any resemblance to actual persons or events is purely coincidental.

Published by: Deep Water Publishing
                     PO Box 140831
                     Garden City, Idaho 83714

Broadside Cartoons Website: www.navybroadside.com

ISBN-13: 978-1-881651-20-8
ISBN-10: 1-881651-20-7

Library of Congress Control Number: 2006930197

10 9 8 7 6 5 4 3 2 1

Broadside ® is a registered trademark of Jeff Bacon.

The author wishes to thank Howard Cohen, Craig Lilly, and Andy Kraft for their editorial support and advice; and Becky who has made every one of these last twenty years so wonderful for me.

Foreword

Jeff Bacon's cartoons show us beyond a doubt that he knows his Sailors. With precision and impartiality, they have captured the daily moments of silliness that mark every specialty in the Navy. Jeff has made us laugh at each other and, when our turn comes, to ante up and laugh at ourselves. And although he can always find the chink in our armor, he has steadfastly exhibited the ability to expose without exploiting. For two decades, *Broadside* has been a reminder for us to take only our mission seriously—not ourselves.

HMCM(FMF) Mark T. Hacala, USN
Director, Education Institute, United States Navy Memorial

The first Broadside

Navy Times
March 24, 1986

I dunno...it's got to be around here somewhere.

Dedication

After the attacks on September 11, 2001, a close friend of mine at the Pentagon told me that I needed to do a special cartoon - one that not only showed respect for our fallen comrades, but also displayed determination and a sense of resolve. The result was this cartoon.

Since then, many of our brethren have been engaged in the continuing struggle to defend the liberties we enjoy. Throughout the history of this great nation, the men and women in uniform have always been the first to answer the call, to go in harm's way, to put their lives on the line to preserve all we hold dear. This book is dedicated to them - to you.

Well-trained after countless drills, the supply officers quickly assume their battle stations.

A Dining Out, fresh rolls, wine for dipping, and an Admiral at the podium. For one tragic moment, it all made sense.

Embarrassing submarine moments

After 47 uneventful duty days, the Command Duty Officer's number comes up.

Ted attends his first wives' club meeting.

Fifteen seconds after the Admiral's words, "Ask me anything, anything at all."

A common scene in the detailers' parking lot

How to mess with a submariner's mind

The few, the proud...the Musician School Drill Instructors

The Holy Helo. Faith in the true sense of the word.

Career Day at Surface Warfare Officers School

Let me get this straight. They put us in these solid steel vehicles that weigh, oh...say 50 tons. Then we drive them off a perfectly good ship into a hundred fathoms of water. We miraculously bob to the top and drive safely to shore. You go first.

The final stage of a bad qual board

The day "Moonshade" tried to crash a SEAL/UDT head shaving party

The Marine Corps Technology Insertion Squad

Find the helo pilot in this picture

Why the Army runs PSYOPS

A bad idea about to get worse

Peer pressure at the LSO platform

Ill-advised April Fools' Day joke

It looked like another long night for the "Fighting Nukes from Orlando."

Another hazard of chewing tobacco

On a 98-degree day in the Indian Ocean, MS3 Howe pulls out the snowball he hid away 28,000 miles ago.

XO group therapy

What department heads don't see

Why the Aerographers lock up the balloon room

Another day at Legal Officers' School

How to know you're out of the loop

Lunch time at the Navy Leadership School

Deep inside enemy territory, Armstrong was beset by an uncontrollable case of the nervous giggles

33

THERE YOU HAVE IT! PUT A SURFACE WARRIOR IN A ROOM LONG ENOUGH WITH NO JOB, NO RESPONSIBILITIES, NO TASKING... AND EVENTUALLY HE'LL FIGURE OUT A WAY TO WORK WEEKENDS.
SATURDAY
Bacon ©2001

LET ME SEE IF I CAN SUMMARIZE OUR DISCUSSION. YOU'RE MARRIED WITH CHILDREN AND I'M SINGLE. YOU HAD DUTY LAST CHRISTMAS AND I TOOK LEAVE. WHAT WAS THE OTHER THING? THERE WAS SOMETHING ELSE... OH THAT'S RIGHT! I OUTRANK YOU.
Bacon ©2005

SNIFF

SO HOW COME YOU DON'T SELL DIET SODAS ANY MORE?
WE HAD TO RE-STOCK 'EM ALL THE TIME... SO WE ELIMINATED THE PROBLEM.
SODA
SODA
SODA
SODA
SODA
Bacon ©2001

A night out with the jet jocks and helo pilots

THERE'S THE PROBLEM.
THERE'S THE PROBLEM.
C.H.T.
DISCHARGE
C.H.T.
PUSH TO START
ON OFF
Bacon©2006

THIS BRIEF HAS ABSOLUTELY NO SUBSTANCE OR VALUE. BUT I'D LIKE TO DRAW YOUR ATTENTION TO THE SLICK GRAPHICS AND ANIMATION YOU'LL SEE THROUGHOUT.
Bacon©2004

LOOK X.O. ... I KNOW IT'S WRITTEN KIND OF POORLY, BUT I JUST DON'T HAVE ANYONE WORKING FOR ME WHO CAN WRITE WELL.
I HAVE THE SAME PROBLEM.
Bacon ©1990 D.C

BRIDGE, CENTRAL...CASUALTY IS TO THE OVERSPEED TRIP ON THE UPPER GONCULATOR CAUSING A FAULT IN THE LUBE OIL GOVERNOR AND REQUIRING A SHUTDOWN OF THE MAIN TURBINE.
RIGHT, TURBINE, WHATEVER. HOW DOES THIS AFFECT MIDRATS?
Bacon ©2005

When F-14 crews carpool

The XO never found his binoculars...although a diver did several years later.

Submarine diplomacy

AAAHH... COMMAND OF AN ARLEIGH BURKE! VERTICAL LAUNCHER, STATE-OF-THE-ART ELECTRONICS... NOBODY CAN TOUCH US! WE'RE MEAN AND LEAN. WE'RE LORDS OF OUR DOMAIN. WE'RE KING OF THE SEAS. WE'RE-
UNDER THE CONTROL OF THE CARRIER. THEY TOLD US TO GO AND RECOVER A BUNCH OF TRASH SOMEBODY THREW OVER THE SIDE.
Bacon ©1996

HELICOPTER PILOT READINESS CONDITIONS:
READY FIFTEEN
READY FIVE
Bacon ©1991 D.H.

REMEMBER HOW MESSY THIS SPACE WAS, X.O.? WELL I PUT A CLEANING DETAIL ON IT HOURS AGO, AND THEY'RE STILL IN THERE! YOU'RE IN FOR A BIG, BIG SURPRISE.
BEEP BEEP
SODA
BACON ©2000

TODAY'S FORECAST: PARTLY SANDY BECOMING MOSTLY SANDY... WITH ISOLATED SANDSTORMS HERE AND HERE.
AFGHANISTAN
PAKISTAN
NAVY
YOU'RE OVERPAID.
BACON ©2001

Never a good sign

IF YOU DIDN'T GET A SEAT, JUST STAND OR SIT IN THE AISLE. OH, AND WE'RE OUT OF COFFEE AND BAGELS.
STRATEGIC PLANNING SEMINAR
BACON ©2005

HEY, MY MAN! CHECK OUT THE NEW KHAKIS.
CALL ME CHIEF.
DUDE! IT'S ME! YOUR OL' SHIPPIE!
CALL ME CHIEF.
AW, C'MON JIMBO... JUST 'CUZ YOU—
SAY, THEY'RE LOOKING FOR A VOLUNTEER TO CLEAN THE HEAD IN THE C.P.O. MESS...
HAVE A NICE DAY, CHIEF.
Congratulations to our new Chiefs!
BACON ©2003

The last COD

CHIEF OF THE BOAT! CHIEF OF THE BOAT! RILEY'S PLAYING SPACE INVADERS ON THE BALLISTIC MISSILE CONSOLE AGAIN!
SQUEALER.
©1995
Bacon

I'VE BEEN HERE THREE HOURS AND NOBODY EVEN KNOWS I'M GONE.
I'VE BEEN HERE THREE WEEKS AND NOBODY EVEN KNOWS I CHECKED ABOARD.
I CAN'T TOP THAT.
SODA
SODA
Bacon ©2004

47

Surface Warrior equivalent of "carrier quals"

"SO WHAT'S THE DIFFERENCE BETWEEN "LAME DUCK" AND "RETIRED ON ACTIVE DUTY"?"

"ATTITUDE. BUT WE TREAT YOU THE SAME EITHER WAY."

48

THE PHASES OF NEW TECHNOLOGY
RESEARCH & DEVELOPMENT
SHF LINK
LCD DISPLAY
TEMPEST APPROVED CASING
FULL DUPLEX FUNCTION KEYS
AUTHORIZATION & ACQUISITION
THEY'RE MADE IN YOUR STATE, SENATOR..
BUY A MILLION OF 'EM.
DISTRIBUTION
HEY! WHERE'S THE PONY ?!
PRACTICAL USE
COFFEE MACHINE DOESN'T WORK.
SMACK
TRY IT NOW.
Bacon ©1996

HE'S PROBABLY NEVER GOTTEN A CANDY BAR FROM THE GREAT SATAN BEFORE.
CANDY
Bacon ©2003

A pivotal moment in the career of John Paul Jones

50

51

J.O. Snooze Alarm
INSTRUCTIONS: XO OPENS STATEROOM DOOR (A), PUSHING CHAIR (B) FORWARD, THRUSTING THE JUNIOR OFFICER (C) TOWARD DESK (D), PRE-LADEN WITH PAST-DUE PAPERWORK (E), GIVING A "NOSE-TO-THE GRINDSTONE" IMAGE.
(FOR ADDED REALISM, TAPE PENCIL (F) TO HAND.)
A
B
C
D
E
F

MY CALLSIGN? WELL, MY OLD SQUADRON CALLED ME THOR... YOU KNOW, GOD OF THUNDER AND WAR AND ALL THAT —
HEY! BINKY! WHEN DID YOU CHECK IN?
Bacon ©1999

Why they put windows in the weather office

Engineering Duty Officer sea stories

OFFICER OF THE DECK! THE SKIPPER JUST FELL OVERBOARD! WHATTAYA WANT ME TO DO?
BONG HIM OFF I GUESS.
Bacon ©1997

GOAL-L-L-L-L-L!
NAVY
NAVY SOCCER?
NAVY RECRUITER.
Bacon ©2001

OKAY, THIS BOX IS THE OFF-LIMITS AREA. WHATEVER YOU DO, DON'T GO THERE!
PORT BRIEF
I'M THERE.
I'M THERE.
I'M THERE.
I'M THERE.
I'M THERE.
I'M THERE.
I'M THERE.
Baca©1994

HEY! HOW COME YOU IGNORED MY EMAIL?
I-I DIDN'T GET YOUR EMAIL, X.O. ...N.M.C.I. MUST HAVE LOST IT.
THAT'S A KEEPER.
Bacon©2005

YOUR MOTHER SAID YOU HAVEN'T SPENT ALL OF YOUR ALLOWANCE. SO GIVE ME BACK WHAT YOU DIDN'T SPEND, AND I'M CUTTING WHAT YOU GET NEXT MONTH TOO.
TWO BILLION MEN IN THE WORLD, AND MOM HAD TO MARRY A COMPTROLLER.
Bacon ©2003

MY CHIEF IS A DUMMY!
WHAT DID YOU TELL THE EXTRA DUTY GUYS TO DO?
PAINT THE BULKHEAD. MAYBE I SHOULD HAVE BEEN MORE SPECIFIC.
Bacon ©2004

The joy of techs

"Hey! Keep your head down! They're gonna fire the shot line any second now!"

Executive Officer's life in a nutshell

Behind the scenes with the Civil Engineer Corps

Submarine barrel rolls

61

62

At long last, the weeks of intensive General Quarters training began to pay off.

63

64

DUDE. YOU STILL ON THE BRIDGE?
I STAND WATCH, THEREFORE I AM.
Bacon ©2004

CORPORAL, WHAT IS YOUR JOB?
SIR! SINCE NOVEMBER TENTH, 1775, THE MARINES HAVE BEEN THE FIRST TO FIGHT IN MAJOR CAMPAIGNS THROUGHOUT THE WORLD. MY JOB IS TO SEEK OUT AND DESTROY THE ENEMY WITH HONOR, COURAGE AND COMMITMENT. AND ALWAYS ATTACK, ATTACK, ATTACK!!
...AND?
FILL UP THIS PUNCH BOWL FOR THE GENERAL'S MARINE CORPS BIRTHDAY PARTY.
Bacon ©1999

The P-3 crew begins its pre-deployment checklist

"FLAPS DOWN" "CHECK"
"LANDING GEAR DOWN" "CHECK"
"PER DIEM CHECKS SIGNED" "CHECK"

An awkward moment at the Pentagon

"MY PROGRAM GOT FUNDED! THEY KILLED OFF SOME LOSER ACQUISITION AND PLUSSED ME UP A HUNDRED MILLION BUCKS!"

"FUNNY... WE JUST LOST A HUNDRED MILLION AND NOW THEY'RE SHUTTING US DOWN."

A slow news day in Afghanistan

It just doesn't matter.

A leading cause of injury at the Pentagon

Supply Corps horror stories

The shortest trial in history

Stand by for shot lines forward.

OH, SURE... MISTER BIG SHOT NAVY GUY. LEMME TELL YOU SOMETHIN... NOAA CORPS OFFICERS ARE BETTER SHIP DRIVERS, BETTER MARINERS, BETTER SAILORS! DEEP DOWN INSIDE YOU KNOW IT, AND I'LL BET YOU'VE LOST A LOTTA SLEEP THINKIN' ABOUT IT!
WHAT'S "NOAA"?
Bacon ©1994

OKAY MEN! THIS IS FOR THE PHOTO SHOOT... SHOW 'EM WE'RE NUKES AND WE MEAN BUSINESS!
Bacon ©1999

Engineers enjoying another great liberty port

The sacred ritual of call sign selection

Late at night in Flight Deck Control

Never volunteer anything.

Once again proving the adage that anything, if discussed long enough, will eventually become a supply problem.

TELL ME I DIDN'T DO ANYTHING STUPID LAST NIGHT.
GETTING A TATTOO ON YOUR FOREHEAD SAYING, "X.O. IS A TYRANT." ...DOES THAT QUALIFY?
Bacon ©2006

♪ WEL-L-L-L... ♪ AND WHAT'S A GIRL LIKE YOU DOING ON A SHIP LIKE THIS?
COMMANDING IT.

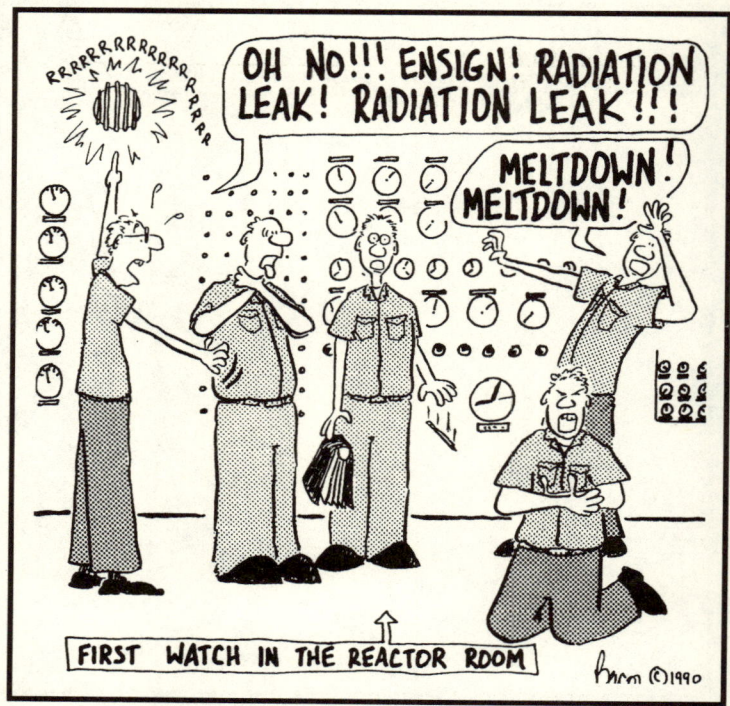

The old "testing the alarms gag" claims another victim.

I USE A LOT OF WHITE SPACE ON MY FITREPS. THE WORDS HAVE MORE IMPACT.
YOU'RE RIGHT. "LOSER" KIND OF JUMPS OUT AT YOU... BEING THE ONLY WORD ON THE PAGE...
Bacon ©2004

I, STATE YOUR NAME, HAVING BEEN APPOINTED AN ENSIGN IN THE U.S. NAVY, DO SOLEMNLY SWEAR THAT I WILL SUPPORT AND DEFEND THE CONSTITUTION OF THE UNITED STATES AGAINST ALL ENEMIES, FOREIGN AND DOMESTIC, THAT I WILL BEAR TRUE FAITH AND ALLEGIANCE TO THE SAME; THAT I TAKE THIS OBLIGATION FREELY, WITHOUT ANY MENTAL RESERVATION OR PURPOSE OF EVASION; THAT I WILL WELL AND FAITHFULLY DISCHARGE THE DUTIES OF THE OFFICE UPON WHICH I AM ABOUT TO ENTER. SO HELP ME GOD.
I, ... CAN'T REMEMBER THE REST... SO HELP ME GOD.
Bacon ©2004

Maritime super heroes

Aboard the U.S.S. Futility

The Coast Guard on patrol

MORNING SIR.
DON'T CALL ME SIR! I WORK FOR A LIVING!
UM, I WAS TALKING TO THE XO, BEHIND YOU.
MORNING.
Bacon ©1998

YN1, GET MY AIDE IN HERE. BEFORE I SIGN THIS, HE NEEDS TO TELL ME WHAT MY STRONG FEELINGS ARE ON THIS MATTER.
ADMIRAL
Bacon ©1998

...HUH.
SOUND THE COLLISION ALARM, AYE!
BACON ©2005

CAREER COUNSELOR
YOU'RE TRYING TO QUIT SMOKING AGAIN, AREN'T YOU.
COME IN. LET'S DISCUSS WHAT'S LEFT OF YOUR MEDIOCRE CAREER.
BACON ©2005

Group Think

Pavlov in the Navy

When Admirals tell jokes

87

When mine hunters hold sweepers

HERE'S YOUR NEW SYSTEM, GANG! IT TOOK OUR SCIENTISTS A FEW YEARS TO DEVELOP, BUT IT'S FINALLY HERE! WELCOME TO THE FUTURE!
DID YOUR SCIENTISTS TELL YOU HOW TO FIT IT THROUGH THE HATCH?
WELCOME TO REALITY.
Bacon ©2002

I CAN'T BELIEVE WE LOST ANOTHER TRAINED DOLPHIN! I MEAN, WHY WOULD THEY WANNA SWIM AWAY? WE TREAT THEM BETTER THAN WE TREAT OUR OWN CREW. BAD LUCK! CHIEF, THIS TASTES GREAT. WHAT IS IT?
MAHI MAHI.
Bacon ©1996

Shower Shoeless Joe

ONE OF THIRTY-SEVEN LIEUTENANTS ?! WOW!
I THINK IT SAYS, "JUST ONE OF THIRTY-SEVEN LIEUTENANTS."
Bacon ©2001

THIS IS A VERY IMPORTANT REPORT. READ IT, STAFF IT, AND DO UP A POWERPOINT BRIEF WITH COLOR HAND-OUTS. THIS IS FOR THE ADMIRAL, SO I WANT QUALITY WORK.
-SIGH-... WHEN DO YOU NEED IT?
IN FIFTEEN MINUTES.
PLOP
Bacon ©2003

"Big John" went through his entire enlistment never knowing he had a hygiene problem.

SEABEE sea stories

A.T.O. with an attitude

ADMIRAL, YOU SAID TO LEAN OVER AND WHISPER IN YOUR EAR TEN MINUTES AFTER THE BRIEF GOT STARTED...
ROGER THAT! I NEED TO GET ON THE HORN WITH PACOM RIGHT AWAY... BETTER WRAP IT UP, SON.
BUT I HAVE THIRTY MORE SLIDES... YES, SIR.
Bacon ©2005

BOY, WE REALLY WANT TO THANK YOU FOR THE SURPRISE INSPECTION! YOU FOUND ENOUGH PROBLEMS TO KEEP US BUSY FOR A LONG, LONG TIME, NOT TO MENTION RUIN MY CAREER... BUT HEY! IT KEEPS US TUNED UP. COME BACK ANY TIME.
YOU'RE HURTING MY HAND, SKIPPER.
Bacon ©2000

If Surface Warriors ran day care

MORNING, MEN!
THEY LOVE ME.
MORNING, LIEUTENANT!
MORON.
LOSER.
Bacon ©2002

VEAL FACTORY
YOU'LL UNDERSTAND AFTER AWHILE.
TAP TAP
TAP TAP
Bacon ©2005

Oil and water. Drinking and driving. Roller-blades and brows.

Seaman Brown is introduced to the Attitude Closet.

The hour glass of death

WHAT DID I SAY ... JUMP THEN PULL! JUMP THEN PULL!
Bacon ©2005

MEN, THERE IS NOTHING SO HONORABLE AS A SAILOR WHO IS WILLING TO SACRIFICE FOR THE GOOD OF HIS SHIPMATES. THE PAGES OF HISTORY ARE FILLED WITH FEATS OF HEROES WHO HAD THE DIGNITY, THE PATRIOTISM, THE MORAL FIBER TO PUT OTHERS AHEAD OF THEMSELVES. NOW, WHAT DOES THAT MEAN TO YOU?
WE'RE CLEANING HEADS AGAIN.
Bacon ©1997

YOU'RE A DISGRACE, CAPTAIN! YOUR SHIP IS A JOKE AND YOU DON'T DESERVE COMMAND AT SEA!
WHAT THE ADMIRAL MEANT TO SAY WAS, "THANKS FOR THE HOSPITALITY AND YOU'RE DOING A GREAT JOB."
BACON ©2000

WHOA, BIG FELLA! HOW BIG'S YOUR WAIST? THINK THE TAPE WILL FIT ALL THE WAY AROUND?
HOW BIG'S YOUR NECK? THINK MY FINGERS WILL FIT ALL THE WAY AROUND?
OKAY! THAT'S A PASS!
BACON ©2001

The harsh reality of the full length photo

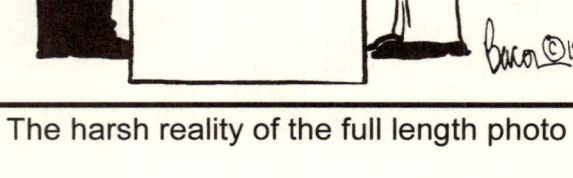

Why Supply Officers aren't eligible for Command-At-Sea

The short-lived Navy/NOAA exchange program

104

Seaman Fabersham's last, tragic, handrail slide

How aviators view surface warfare

YOU WANT TO TAKE OFF EARLY? COME ON, THERE'S NO "I" IN TEAM.
THERE'S NO "U" IN LIBERTY, EITHER... WHICH IS KIND OF THE POINT.
BACON ©2005

HOW'S IT GOING? I JUST CHECKED IN YESTERDAY.
NEW GUY, EH? I THINK I'M SUPPOSED TO TURN OVER ALL OF MY COLLATERAL DUTIES TO YOU...
I CHECKED IN YESTERDAY. I WASN'T BORN YESTERDAY.
BACON ©2003

107

AOCS touch-and-goes

Safety Mishap Bulletin: SA injured by unidentified airborne object resembling Navy boondocker

Beware the end-of-tour detailer

MEET THE OPERATIONS OFFICER. THANKS TO REFRESHER TRAINING, AN UNDERWAY REPLENISHMENT, COUNTLESS FLIGHT OPERATIONS, AND ONE SONAR CONTACT, HE HAS GONE WITHOUT SLEEP FOR TWO DAYS. NOW, AS THE TEMPO SLOWS, HE CAN FINALLY LOOK FORWARD TO A
GOOD N
SLEE
TAO? YOUR RELIEF HAS THE MUMPS.
Bacon ©1990

SKIPPER, WE NEED A NEW BREAK AWAY SONG.
MY ONLY OTHER STREISAND CD IS IN MY CABIN.
LET ME PUT IT ANOTHER WAY...
Bacon ©2003

@*!☆#!@
YOU MAKE ME SICK, YOU KNOW THAT?
YOU CAN'T GET TO ME... I'M TOO STUPID.
Bacon ©2000

WHO THE @*#!★ PUT SHOE POLISH ON MY TOOTHBRUSH!
THINK THINK THINK
Bacon ©2004

113

To the nukes he was known affectionately as "Mr. Pep." To everyone else, unfortunately, he was simply a dweeb.

115

A light moment in the detailer shop

The Marine Corps' first and last attempt at encounter groups

YOU'RE PUTTING ME IN CHARGE? COOL!
THAT'S NOT WHAT I MEAN BY "HEAD CLEANER".
BACON ©2001

BASED ON A TRIANGULATED FIX, NAVIGATION HOLDS US SOMEWHERE IN THIS HUMONGOUS TRIANGLE!
YOU'RE REALLY NOT HELPING.
BACON ©2006

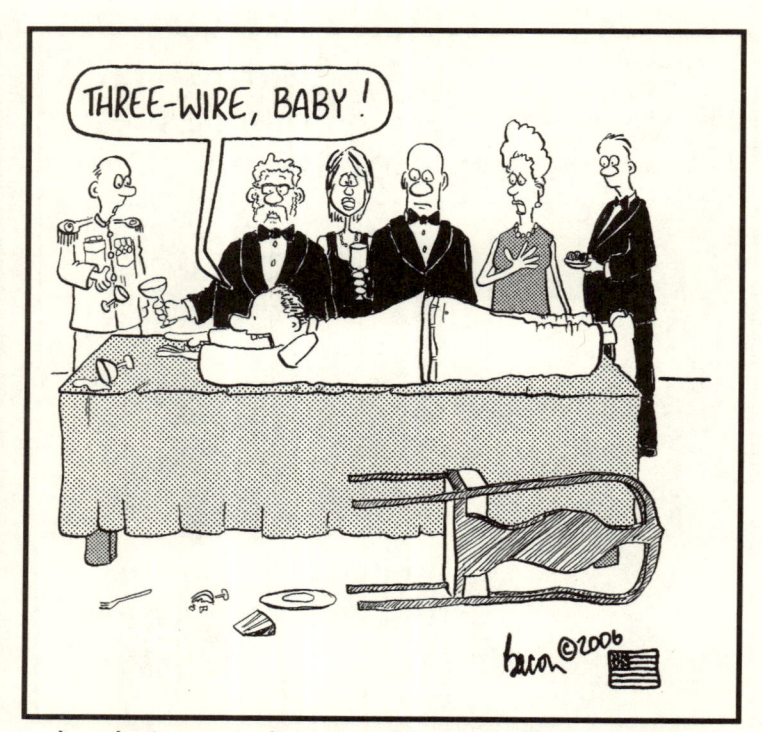

In what was to become his last official act, the Admiral tried to liven up the embassy dinner with "carrier quals."

LET'S GO, FELLA. IT'S ONE OR THE OTHER.
GIVE ME A MINUTE.
SHARP STICKS TO POKE IN YOUR EYE
PENTAGON PROGRAM BRIEF →
Bacon ©2003

BESIDES "WASTE 'EM", HOW ELSE MIGHT YOU DEAL WITH A HOSTILE TAKE-OVER BID?
COLLEGE-AT-SEA BUSINESS 101
?
S.E.A.L.
S.E.A.L.
S.E.A
Bacon ©2004

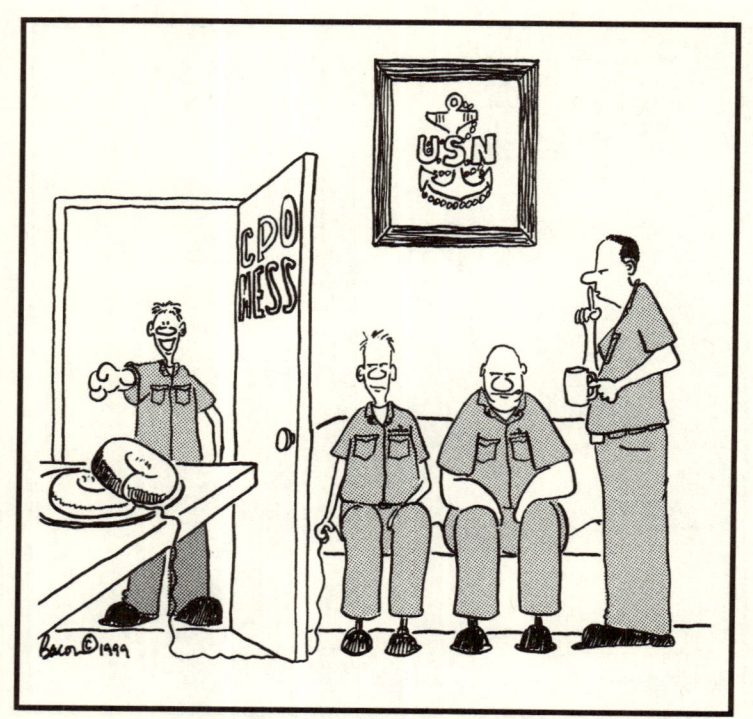

Trolling for Mess Cooks

Death row

HEY, I NEED A RULING. CHIEF SAID SINCE I WAS BEING BOOTED FOR MISCONDUCT, I COULD LAUNCH MY BOONDOCKERS OFF THE NUMBER 2 CATAPULT.
YEAH? SO?
SO IS IT TRUE I HAVE TO BE WEARING 'EM?
Bacon ©1999

OKAY, THAT'S THE MISSION.
OORAH!
HOO-AH!
HOO-YA.
...AHOY?
USMC
Bacon ©2003

Live entertainment appearing daily in the Chiefs' mess

Time management at its finest

In the spirit of process improvement, the weatherman is invited to the Captain's window to verify his forecast.

"YOUR CHOICE. WE CAN TRAIN YOU ON SOME TOUCHY-FEELY GARBAGE, OR WE CAN GO BLOW STUFF UP. WHO WANTS TO BLOW STUFF UP?"

Training Day at EOD headquarters

"I'LL NOW READ MY RETIREMENT ORDERS... AS SOON AS EVERYONE STOPS DANCING AROUND AND GIVING EACH OTHER "HIGH FIVES.""